Weight Struggles?

Don Barnes

Published by Don Barnes, 2024.

LifeWorksInThrees.com

Table of Contents

About the Author

Don Barnes is the founder and author of TRYUNE WORKS!™. He is a lifelong Texan who has traveled extensively while taking a keen interest in human behavior. His curiosity about life and what drives humans led him to the discovery of how life works in threes. He coined this term as the *Tryune Concept.*

Don attended college on an athletic scholarship and then embarked on a 30-year career in the oil and gas industry. During his post O&G days, he got involved in a polar-bonding technology for lubrication and a liquid ozone technology used to replace chlorine for water treatment.

Along the way, he worked on his Tryune discovery, in hopes of someday sharing his findings with those struggling unnecessarily in life. What Don surmised from 40+ years of R&D was that people were struggling unnecessarily in life because they were not aware that "life works in threes." People, for the most part, are living their lives by chance rather than by choice.

From this, he began focusing on the "mechanics of life" which shows formulas for success with subjects such as *life, health, money, purpose and so forth.* When humans are able to grasp the Tryune Concept, they can apply the formula of topics that interest them and begin eliminating the struggle. This epiphany is what triggered his Tryune venture and is now on the path of sharing this amazing discovery with all who desire to improve on their lives.

Don currently resides in Southern California and Texas while overseeing his businesses and investments.

Life Works in Threes™

When I was a kid growing up, no one sat me down and said, "Okay Don, I'm going to show you how life works so that you can navigate your way through adulthood." I graduated from school, got married and went about my way with the "learn as you go" concept. It was kind of like putting together a backyard swing set without a set of instructions. Lots of frustration and do-overs, for sure!

My discovery of the "triune" word and noticing how things come together in threes is really what set me off on researching that maybe "life comes in three" ...sort of a mechanical approach to managing life, if you will. I combed the libraries and bookstores for information on this and found one book on the subject that was written back in 1951. The author's name was John S. Arant.

What Mr. Arant had to say is this "For lack of a better name, I have called this *The Triangle of Triumph* and therefore, consistent with the name, since most of these conclusions are built on the geometric figure of the triangle." He continued "All Life and all lives are seated in, and circumscribed by, the triangle. The Author and Source and Director of all life is Himself triune in character – Father, Son, and Holy Spirit. Man is of triple nature – body, mind, and spirit – and within those three there are many triangles – desires, development, decay; intellect, will, sensibilities. Of this "paced interlude in the midst of eternity" which we call time there is the triangle of Past, Present, and Future. Space – that limitless and measureless element of the physical universe – is best known in terms of Height, Breadth, and Depth. Try building yourself some triangles along the lines of your Will, your Work, your Way – You will find some interesting angles.

So, for the first time, I realized that life is designed in a mechanical way to come in threes. That means you don't have to rely on wishing and hoping things turn out okay. You can actually look at the three parts that a particular thing is made of and then apply them to get what you're wanting. Like a three-ingredient recipe or a combination lock. With a combination lock, you need the three exact numbers to unlock the lock...otherwise you will continue to struggle.

Some 40 years later, I accumulated things that work in threes and that's when I knew I needed to share this with anyone wanting answers. To have success/harmony in your life, just apply the three parts of an area you're working on, and things will fall into place. I also learned that the recipe for success with just about anything is by doing these three things, consistently – THINK positively, SPEAK positively and ACT positively. For example, if I want to be a successful artist. I would think to myself "I can do this because I have the talent." Then I would speak it this way "Yes, I am working on my art degree and plan to do portraits professionally." Finally, I would act on that by taking art classes and continue crafting my skill. Eventually, I will see the positive results/success I'm looking for.

Conversely, if I think positively but speak negatively...it will cancel out. Or if I speak positively but have no positive action going on...nothing will happen.

I looked up "How Life Works" and "The Mechanics of Life" and these are really talking about the biology of how our cells work and other chemistry. TRYUNE WORKS! teaches that life is kind of like building blocks. Pick a topic you may be struggling with. See the three parts that topic consists of and then start applying them...on a consistent basis. That will help you overcome the struggle and get you back in harmony/success with how life works.

For 30+ years I was a golf instructor (by accident). My two kids had some success playing junior golf and so friends and neighbors would ask me to show them and their kids how to play golf successfully. From all of this, I got pretty good at watching golfers on the driving range and could spot right away why they were struggling with hitting bad golf shots. I was able to do that because I knew the three steps to hitting good golf shots. I learned them from studying golf and played for several decades. I "broke the code" for me so to speak.

So now you know that life works in threes. You can live your life *by choice* rather than *by chance* and that my friend... is the key to a fulfilling life.

Introduction

Finding balance in weight management is like navigating a tasty, yet tricky, buffet of health choices. It's tempting to dive headfirst into extreme diets or exercise routines, but **moderation** is the secret sauce for sustainable success. Think of it as creating a delicious recipe for a healthier you, where every ingredient plays a vital role.

Firstly, let's talk about diets. Instead of hopping on the latest fad diet rollercoaster, aim for **a balanced plate**. Incorporate a variety of colorful fruits, veggies, lean proteins, and whole grains. It's not about deprivation; it's about making mindful choices that nourish your body and satisfy your taste buds. Remember, a little indulgence here and there is perfectly fine – it's all about the big picture.

Next up, exercise. While hitting the gym seven days a week might seem like the fast track to fitness, it's essential to give your body the rest and recovery it craves. Mix things up with different activities you enjoy, whether it's yoga, dancing, or a leisurely stroll in the park. **Consistency is key**, but so is listening to your body and giving it the TLC it deserves. By finding the sweet spot between pushing yourself and taking it easy, you'll build a healthy relationship with exercise that lasts a lifetime. So, remember, when it comes to weight management, **steer clear of extremes**, and embrace the beauty of balance.

My discovery of How Life Works in Threes

Before we dive into weight struggles and how to overcome them, let me share my discovery of the Tryune Concept and *how life works in threes.* It all began in the summer of 1982.

I grew up with parents who treated everyone with decency and respect. My three older sisters and I were raised in a home that was "middle-class traditional." We lived in modest homes in different small towns, attended school and church on a regular basis and celebrated all the traditional holidays. Eventually we settled during the spring of 1964 in the big city of Houston, Texas. I'll never forget the vastness of the city and hearing sirens from police cars, fire trucks and ambulances on a regular basis. I was excited and scared at the same time.

Once settled in this fast-paced city, I finished my growing-up years with an academic diploma and sweetheart intact. I got a job, bought a car, got married, bought a house and produced two beautiful babies in a span of about 5 years. Talk about having to grow up fast!

Things went from great in my childhood to absolute misery in my young adulthood. I began to struggle with my job because deep down I just hated what I was doing. This problem created a snowball effect because soon after, my weight, my finances, my relationships, my happiness and everything else worth saving was going down the drain. I eventually hit a level of frustration that I had never experienced before and didn't know how to get out of it. My cry for help was for anyone or anything to come to my rescue. I just ran out of solutions for my situation.

This is when my discovery happened.

One night shortly after my meltdown, while sleeping soundly, the word "triune" began to softly pound in my head like a mantra. I woke up a little startled and decided to go look up the word in my favorite dictionary (this was WAY before Google.) The definition said '**triune** (try-une) – 1) a group of three things; united. 2) Being 3 in 1 such as *humans are mental, physical and spiritual.* I scratched my head, got a glass of water and went back to bed.

The next day while driving around town, I began thinking about things that I was taught in my younger years that came in threes. My Boy Scout manual taught that to have **character**, I needed to be *1) physically strong, 2) mentally awake and 3) morally straight.* My high school football coach would say emphatically "If you want to be **a good football player**, you have to be *1) mobile 2) agile and 3) hostile!*" My first sales manager shared with me that to be **a successful salesman**, I needed to have *1) sales skills, 2) product knowledge and 3) a good image.*

"Hmm", I thought, "wonder if there are other examples out there of things that work in threes?" So, some 40 years later, I have researched and discovered that many, many things work in threes. What this message was telling me is that to achieve success or balance in any significant area of my life, the three things that area consisted of had to be present continuously. That's when I had my epiphany. This discovery was telling me the secret to how life <u>really</u> works.

Tryune is a play on the word "triune" as an invitation to "try" this concept. Furthermore, we do not say that life <u>only</u> works in threes. Life also works in ones, twos, fours and so on. What has been observed though is that the many things significant to life, just so happen to come and work in threes. That's what is being shared in this book.

Now, you are about to see 40+ years of research and proof that life works in threes. I did not make up any of these topics. I invite you to research them on the internet, as I did, to validate what is written here. There are some interesting facts that most of us have never realized...until now.

How Life Works in Threes (around 200 examples)

<u>**LIFE**</u>

Humans consist of *body, mind and soul.*

A human's basic needs are *health, income and provisions.*

A human's basic wants are *comfort, gain and approval.*

Our minds are made up of the *conscious, the subconscious and the unconscious.*

Philosophy explains *the id, the ego and superego.*

Atoms consist of *protons, neutrons and electrons.*

Motion is explained by *three basic laws.*

Science falls under three main branches: *natural, social and formal sciences*

Time is *past, present and future...*at the same time.

Electricity consists of *ohms, amperes and voltage.*

Music's basic elements are *duration, pitch and timbre.*

Democracy is a government *of the people, by the people and for the people.*

U.S. branches of government are *the judicial, the executive and the legislative.*

Armed Forces protect us on *land, air and sea.*

Environmentally, we are asked *to reduce, recycle and re-use.*

The news program gives us *the news, sports and conditions.*

Our days consist of *morning, afternoon and evening.*

Three months in each season of the year

Our main meals are known as *breakfast, lunch and dinner.*

A balanced diet consists of *good proteins, carbohydrates and fats.*

Traditional Family consists of *father, mother, and child(ren)*

<u>SCIENCES</u>

Three major branches of natural science – *(physical, earth/ space and life sciences)*

Three major branches of modern physics - *(classical, relativistic, quantum)*

Three major branches of biology *(botany, zoology, microbiology)*

Three spatial dimensions: *height* (up/down), *width* (left/ right) and *depth* (forwards/backwards)

Three-gauge bosons (photon, gluon, W&Z bosons)

Three types of elementary particles *(leptons, quarks, gauge bosons)*

Three quarks in every proton *(two "up" and one "down")*

Three primary colors of light *(red, green, blue)*

Three color tone properties *(hue, value, chroma)*

Three laws of motion (*Newton's laws*)

Three laws of planetary motion (*Kepler's laws*)

Three layers of the Sun's interior (*core, radiative zone, convective zone*)

Three layers of the Sun's atmosphere (*photosphere, chromosphere, corona*)

Three types of meteorites (*iron, stony iron, stony*)

Three types of galaxy shapes (*elliptical, spiral, irregular*)

Three substances of the universe (*normal matter, 'dark matter', 'dark energy'*)

Three phases of the moon (*new moon, first quarter, full moon*)

Three planetary regions (*temperate, sub-tropical, tropical*)

Three layers of the Earth (*crust, mantle, core*)

Three components of an ecosystem (*producers, consumers, decomposers*)

Three types of rocks (*igneous, sedimentary, metamorphic*)

Three types of fossil fuels (*coal, crude oil, natural gas*)

Three hydrological processes (*evaporation, condensation, precipitation*)

Three basic types of (meteorological) precipitation (*liquid, freezing, frozen*)

Three types of substances *(mono-constituent, multi-constituent, UVCB)*

Three phases of (normal) matter *(solid, liquid, gas)*

Three types of covalent chemical bonds *(single, double and triple bonds)*

Three isotopes of hydrogen *(protium, deuterium, tritium)*

Three atoms in each molecule of water *(two hydrogen atoms and an oxygen atom)*

Three endings to salts *(-ide, -ite, -ate)*

Three requirements for fire *(fuel, oxygen, heat)*

Three nucleotide bases in a genetic codon

Three domains of life *(archaea, bacteria and eukaryotes)*

Three major groups of flowering plants *(monocots, eudicots, magnolids)*

Three major functions that are basic to plant growth and development: *(photosynthesis* [making sugars], *respiration* [metabolizing those sugars], and *transpiration* [water vapor loss]

Three things that the chlorophyll in plants needs for photosynthesis to take place: *(sunlight, carbon dioxide and water)*

Transpiration serves three roles: *(cooling the plant, moving minerals* and *sugars through the plant,* and *maintaining the turgidity pressure* [stiffness] *of the plant's cells)*

Three parts of an insect's body *(head, thorax, abdomen)*

<u>BIOLOGY</u>

Three types of cones in the retina, relating to the three primary colors

Three semi-circular canals in the ear *(lateral, anterior, posterior)*

Three sections in the ear *(outer, middle, inner)*

Three ossicles in the middle ear *(malleus, incus, stapes)*

Three segments to each limb *(proximal, mid, distal)*

Three bones in each arm *(humerus, radius, ulna)*

Three joints in the arm *(shoulder, elbow, wrist)*

Three joints in the leg *(hip, knee, ankle)*

Three joints in the elbow *(humeroulnar, humeroradial, proximal radioulnar)*

Three functional compartments in the knee joint *(the femoropatellar, medial femorotibial* and *lateral femorotibial articulations)*

Three types of fibrous joints *(sutures, gomphoses, syndesmoses)*

Three types of bone in each hand (*carpals, metacarpals, phalanges*)

Three types of bone in each foot (*tarsals, metatarsals, phalanges*)

Three bones (phalanges) in each finger and in each toe (*proximal, intermediate, distal*)

Three layers of skin (*dermis, epidermis, hypodermis*)

Three components of a cell (*cell membrane, nucleus, cytoplasm*)

Three types of blood vessels (*arteries, veins, capillaries*)

Three types of blood cells [*red* (erythrocytes), *white* (leukocytes), *platelets* (thrombocytes)]

Three processes of the intestinal tract (*ingestion, digestion, excretion*)

Three germ layers (*Endoderm, Mesoderm, Ectoderm*)

Three parts of a human tooth (*crown, neck, root*)

Three organs of otolaryngology (*ear, nose, throat*)

Three major body systems (*digestive, circulatory, respiratory*)

Three parts to a neuron: (*soma* [*cell body*], *axon, dendrites*)

Three main parts of the brain (*forebrain, midbrain, hindbrain*)

Three parts of the forebrain *(cerebrum, thalamus, hypothalamus)*

Three parts of the midbrain *(colliculi, tegmentum, cerebral peduncles)*

Three parts of the hindbrain *(cerebellum, pons, medulla)*

Three membranes enclosing the brain *(dura mater, arachnoid, pia mater)*

The brain operates on three levels: *consciously* (for cognitive thought and declarative memory); *subconsciously* (for pre-planned actions and procedural memory); and *unconsciously* (for breathing, heart beating, etc.)

Our conscious mind is fed from three sources: *our senses* (which can be fooled); *our memory* (which is flawed); and *our imagination* (which is inventive)

Three aspects of the human mind *(memory, intellect, will)*

Three parts of the human personality *(id, ego, superego)*

The sum of human capacity consists of three abilities *(thought, word and deed)*

Three times of man *(birth, life, death)*

Three periods of the Gait Cycle *(initial double limb support, single limb support, and terminal double limb support)*

<u>MUSIC</u>

Three types of musical notes *(sharps, flats, naturals)*

Three aspects of a song (*lyrics, melody, rhythm*)

Three types of musical chords (*root, third, fifth*)

MATHEMATICS

Three types of a real number (*positive, negative, zero*)

Three parts to any arithmetic operation: for addition: *augend, addend and sum* - for subtraction: *minuend, subtrahend and difference* - for multiplication: *multiplicand, multiplier and product* - for division: *dividend, divisor and quotient*

Three laws of arithmetic operations (*commutative, associative, distributive*)

Three types of equivalence relation (*reflexivity, symmetry, transitivity*)

Three types of symmetry operations (*translation, rotation, reflection*)

Three geometries (*Euclidean, spherical, hyperbolic*)

The number 3 is the basis of an entire branch of mathematics, called trigonometry (from the Greek *trigonon* "triangle" + *metron* "measure")

Three trigonometric functions (*sine, cosine, tangent*)

Three types of average (*mean, mode, median*)

GRAMMAR

Three logical operators (*AND, OR and NOT*)

Three laws of logic (*identity, noncontradiction, excluded middle*)

Three parts of a logical syllogism (*major premise, minor premise, conclusion*)

Three grammatical parts to a sentence (*subject, verb, complement*)

Three persons in grammar [*1st person* (I/we), *2nd* (you or your), *3rd* (he/she/it/they)]

Three genders in grammar [*masculine* (he/him), *feminine* (she/her), *neuter* (it)]

Three forms of comparison in grammar [*positive, comparative* (more, -er), *superlative* (most, -est)]

Three cases in (English) grammar [*subjective/nominative* (he), *objective/accusative* (him) and *possessive/genitive* (his)]

Three parts of a narrative (*beginning, middle, end*)

Components of an essay (*introduction, body, conclusion*)

Elements of a rhetorical appeal (*ethos, pathos, logos*)

Aspects of a story (*plot, characters, setting*)

<u>RELIGION</u>

The Creator – *omniscient, omnipotent, omnipresent*

Christian God – *Father, Son, Holy Spirit*

Jesus – *The Way, The Truth, The Life*

Ancient Near East- *Qudshu, Astarte, Anat*

Classical Antiquity – Many dieties came in threes

Hinduism – Para Brahman is *Brahma, Visnu, Shiva*

Ancient Celtic Cultures – *many example of triad dieties*

Buddhism – *The three jewels*

Taoism – *The three pure ones*

Islam – *Fear, Hope and Love*

Baha'i - *Intention, Power and Action*

Confucianism – *Benevolence, Wisdom and Courage*

<u>OTHER TRIUNE EXAMPLES</u>

3 Coins in a Fountain

3 Days of the Condor

3 Miles in a League

3 Goals in a Hat Trick

3 Piece Suit

3 Feet in a Yard

3 Books in Lord of the Rings

3 Ring Circus

3 Ships of Christopher Columbus

3 Sheets to the Wind

3 Books in a Trilogy

3 Wheels on a Tricycle

3 Wise Men

3-Legged Race

3 Ring Circus

3-Wheeler

3 Cornered Hat

3 Dimensional

3 Musketeers

3 R's (reading, 'riting, 'rithmatic)

3 Sides of a triangle

3 Races in the Triple Crown (horse racing)

3 Angles in a Triangle

3 Trimesters in a Pregnancy

3 Flavors in Neapolitan Ice Cream

3 Stars in Orion's belt

3 Barleycorns in an Inch

3 Hands on a Clock (with the Seconds Hand)

3 Colors in a Flag

3 Minute Egg

3 Great Pyramids at Giza

3 Holes in a Bowling Ball

3 Colors in a Set of Traffic Lights

3 Minutes in a Boxing Round

3 Teaspoons in a Tablespoon

3 Legs on a Stool

3 Monastic Vows (Obience, Stability, Conversatio Morum)

3 Body Types: Endomorph, Mesomorph, Ectomorph

3 Ring Notebooks

3 Germ layers: Endoderm, Mesoderm, Ectoderm

3 Species of Homo: Homo habilis, Homo erectus, Homo sapiens

3 Basic parts of a camera: Lens, Shutter, Sensor

3 Stages of a Project lifecycle: initiation, planning, execution

The Truth, The Whole Truth and Nothing but the Truth

Life, Liberty and the Pursuit of Happiness

Hear no Evil, See no Evil, Speak no Evil

National motto of France/Haiti: Liberty, Equality, Fraternity

Paper, Rock, Scissors

Ready, Aim, Fire

On Your mark, Get Set, Go

Olympic medals of gold, silver, bronze

Types of joints (ball & socket, hinge, pivot)

Stages of a rocket launch (launch, orbit, re-entry)

Parts of a joke (setup, delivery, punchline)

Primary components of a transistor (emitter, base, collector)

Primary components of an airplane (fuselage, wings, empennage)

Basic components of a computer: CPU, memory, storage

Three phases in the development of technology (*eotechnic* [*mechanical*], *paleotechnic* [*steam-powered*] and *neotechnic* [*electric-powered*]

Communication systems require three components (*transmitter, channel, receiver*)

The list goes on. See if you can find more examples as they are everywhere in our universe! Now that you know that life works in threes (with proof!), we can begin to apply this concept to whatever topics we want.

So, to overcome struggles with weight, we need to apply the three areas that weight management consists of – MOOD, INTAKE and OUTPUT. Let's get started!

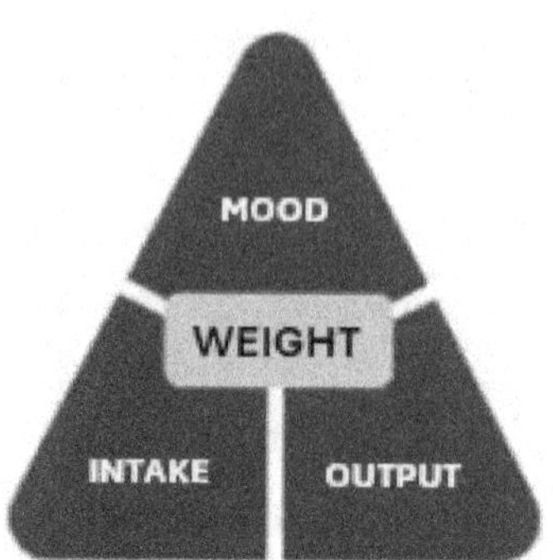
MOOD
WEIGHT
INTAKE
OUTPUT

WEIGHT

I'm going to share a true story that you can verify the next time you go to a football game. On the internet and meeting with weight trainers, I would often hear that "You are this height so this needs to be your weight." Apparently, way back in time, someone came up with a weight chart and said "If this is your height then this should be your weight +/-." Well, I'm calling BS on that and here's why.

I was a jock who played football among other sports and one thing I always knew is that guys that were the same height did not necessarily carry the same weight. Case in point: when you look at a football roster/program at a game, the height and weight of the players are typically listed. So, let's look at football players who are 6' 2" tall in height. There are linemen who can weigh anywhere from 250 lbs. to 300+ lbs. And they are in good shape. Then you have linebackers who are the same height, and they weigh around 225 lbs. They too are in great shape. Finally, you have the wide receivers. These guys run like gazelles, and they will typically weigh between 170 to 190 lbs. You see my point? Three different players at the same height, in excellent shape and fall into a different weight class. So, if you have a weight chart...throw it out. Besides weight only matters in football and boxing. Oh yeah, and sumo wrestling.

What matters is how we feel. If we're feeling sluggish, then maybe cut back on carbs and do some exercise to burn calories. If we're feeling weak, then maybe add some carbs and meat protein to get lean. Going to your doctor and getting his/her opinion is the most practical thing to do here. Many different factors can go into weight change so doing your vitals and finding out what might be missing allows you to know where you stand.

Instead of focusing on how much we weigh, let's focus on what weight feels the best for us. Agree?

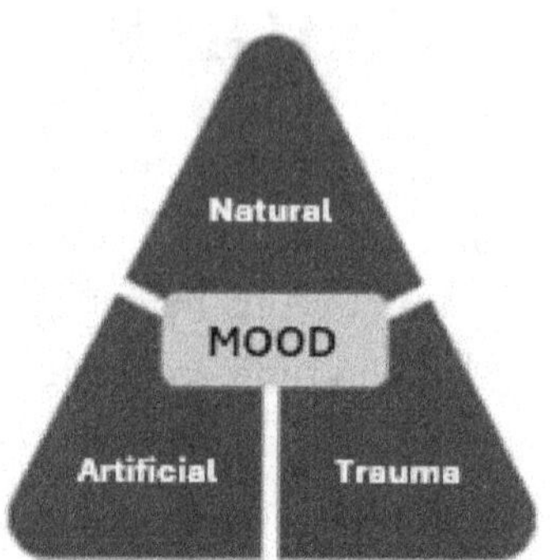
Natural
MOOD
Artificial
Trauma

MOOD

Ah, mood swings – those unpredictable mood dance parties that can leave us feeling like we're on a rollercoaster ride! But fear not, understanding the reasons behind these emotional twists and turns can help us navigate them with a bit more grace.

First up, let's chat about **hormones.** Yep, those sneaky little chemicals can wreak havoc on our moods faster than you can say "mood swing." From puberty to pregnancy to that time of the month, our bodies are constantly playing hormone hopscotch, and sometimes they miss a step. So, if you find yourself going from happy camper to grumpy bear for no apparent reason, hormones might just be the culprit.

Next on the list: **stress.** Ah, stress – the not-so-silent saboteur of our emotional equilibrium. Whether it's deadlines at work, relationship woes, or just life throwing curveballs, stress can turn our emotions into a topsy-turvy tornado. When our stress levels skyrocket, our moods can go haywire, leaving us feeling like we're riding an emotional rollercoaster with no end in sight.

Last but certainly not least, **sleep** (or lack thereof). Yep, the power of a good night's sleep – it's like magic for our moods. But when we skimp on shut-eye, our emotional stability can take a nosedive faster than you can say "lights out." From crankiness to tears to feeling like a walking zombie, sleep deprivation can turn even the most cheerful souls into grumpy gusses. So, if you're feeling like a moody mess, it might be time to cozy up with your favorite pillow and catch some Z's.

Our moods can trigger our eating habits. If we can treat the cause rather than the symptom, then we can gain control of our habits. Once again, a visit to a medical doctor can help with what might be going on.

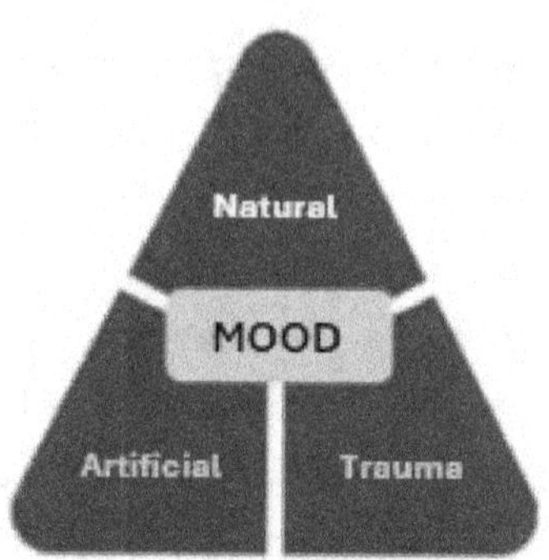

Natural
MOOD
Artificial
Trauma

Natural

Our bodies are like intricate machines, and just like any well-oiled engine, they come equipped with their own set of natural cues and signals that influence our eating habits. So, let's take a peek under the hood and explore a few of these fascinating mechanisms.

First, the **hunger hormones**. Meet ghrelin and leptin – the dynamic duo responsible for letting our brains know when it's time to fuel up or hit the brakes. Ghrelin, our hunger hormone, is like the little gremlin in our stomachs, growling and grumbling to let us know it's time to eat. Meanwhile, leptin plays the role of the satisfied customer, signaling to our brains when we've had our fill. But just like any superhero sidekick duo, these hormones can sometimes get their wires crossed, leading to cravings, overeating, or skipping meals altogether.

Next on the menu: **blood sugar levels**. Ah, the sweet symphony of glucose coursing through our veins – it's like a delicately choreographed dance between energy and appetite. When our blood sugar levels dip too low, our bodies send out an SOS signal for a quick energy fix, often in the form of sugary snacks or carb-loaded treats. But while these quick fixes might provide temporary relief, they can send our blood sugar levels on a rollercoaster ride of highs and lows, leaving us feeling hungry, hangry, and downright out of sorts.

Reaction to events. When life throws curveballs our way, our bodies kick into fight-or-flight mode, flooding our systems with adrenaline and cortisol. While these stress hormones might have helped our ancestors outrun hungry predators, they can wreak havoc on our modern-day eating habits, leading to mindless munching, emotional eating, or even loss of appetite. So, if you find yourself reaching for that pint of ice cream after a long day, don't beat yourself up – it's just your body's way of trying to cope with the chaos.

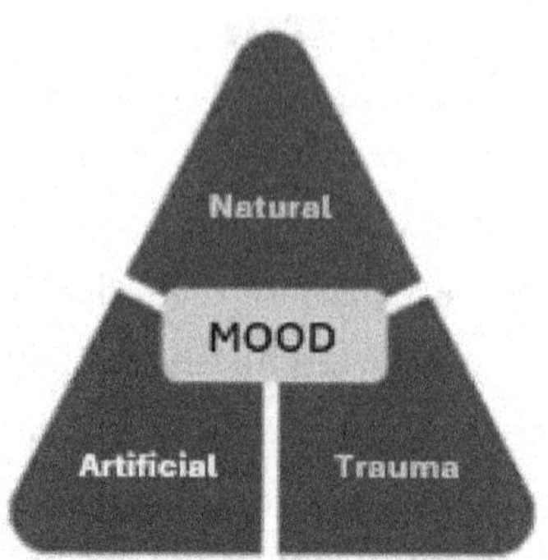

Natural
MOOD
Artificial
Trauma

Artificial

Let's dive into the curious world of mood-altering substances and their sneaky influence on our eating habits! From caffeine to alcohol to the occasional sweet treat, these substances can have quite the impact on our relationship with food.

Caffeine – that magical elixir that turns sleepy bears into productive powerhouses. While a morning cup of joe might be just what the doctor ordered to kickstart your day, too much caffeine can send your appetite on a wild ride. Think of it like revving up your engine without any fuel – your body's ready to go, but your hunger signals get lost in the shuffle. So, if you find yourself skipping breakfast or reaching for snacks instead of meals, it might be time to dial back on the caffeine and tune in to your body's natural rhythm.

Alcohol. The social lubricant of choice for many a merry maker. While a glass of wine or a cold beer can be a delightful addition to any gathering, alcohol can also throw a wrench into your eating habits. Not only does it pack a punch in the calorie department, but it can also lower inhibitions and lead to mindless munching. So, if you find yourself raiding the fridge after a night out on the town, it might be time to pace yourself and reach for a glass of water instead.

Sugar. The sweet siren song that calls to us from the depths of the pantry. While a little sweetness can brighten even the dreariest of days, too much sugar can send our taste buds into overdrive and leave us craving more. From sugary snacks to sweetened beverages, these sneaky culprits can wreak havoc on our eating habits, leading to sugar highs and crashes that leave us feeling drained and irritable. So, if you find yourself reaching for that candy bar or soda pop, try swapping it out for a healthier alternative like fruit or a handful of nuts. Your body and your taste buds will thank you!

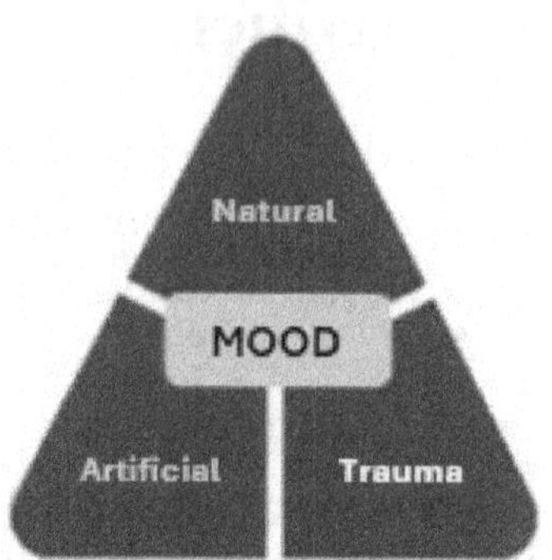

Natural
MOOD
Artificial
Trauma

Trauma

Let's shine a light on the often-overlooked connection between trauma and our eating habits. When we experience trauma, whether it's a single significant event or a series of challenging circumstances, it can cast a long shadow over our relationship with food.

Trauma can disrupt our sense of safety and stability, sending our nervous systems into overdrive. In times of stress, our bodies often crave comfort and familiarity, and for many of us, food provides just that. Whether it's reaching for a pint of ice cream after a tough day or mindlessly munching on snacks to numb the pain, food can become a source of solace in the midst of chaos.

Control. When our lives feel chaotic and unpredictable, we often seek out ways to regain a sense of control, and for some of us, that control manifests in our eating habits. Whether it's rigidly restricting food intake or turning to binge eating as a coping mechanism, our relationship with food can become a battleground where we attempt to assert dominance over our circumstances.

Emotional eating. When we're grappling with difficult emotions, whether it's sadness, anger, or anxiety, food can become a quick and easy way to numb the pain. But while emotional eating might provide temporary relief, it often leaves us feeling even worse in the long run, trapped in a cycle of guilt and shame. So, if you find yourself turning to food as a way to cope with trauma, know that you're not alone, and there are healthier ways to navigate these challenging emotions.

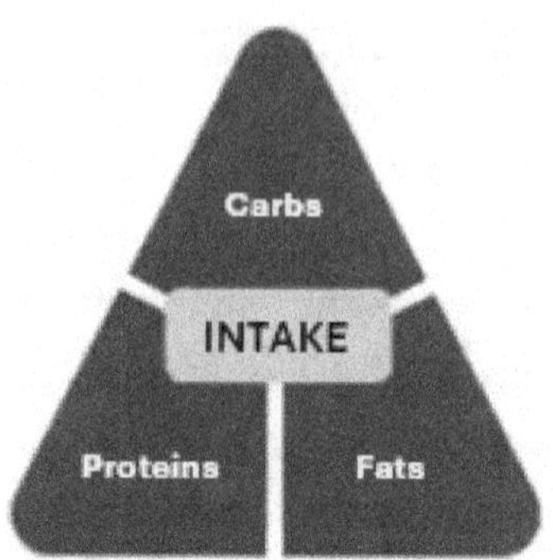

Carbs
INTAKE
Proteins
Fats

INTAKE

Maintaining a healthy weight is like finding the perfect balance on a seesaw – it's all about nourishing your body with the right foods while still enjoying the occasional treat. So, let's chat about some delicious and nutritious goodies that can help keep your weight in check.

Fruits and veggies – the superheroes of the food world! Packed with vitamins, minerals, and fiber, these colorful gems are like nature's multivitamin. Whether you're crunching on carrots, slicing into strawberries, or whipping up a leafy green salad, fruits and veggies should be the stars of your plate. Not only do they keep you feeling full and satisfied, but they also provide a wide range of nutrients to keep your body humming along like a well-oiled machine.

Lean proteins. From chicken and fish to beans and tofu, protein is the building block of a healthy diet. Not only does it help keep you feeling full and satisfied, but it also plays a crucial role in repairing and rebuilding your body's tissues. So, whether you're firing up the grill for some juicy chicken breasts or simmering a pot of hearty lentil soup, make sure to include plenty of protein in your meals to help maintain muscle mass and keep your metabolism revved up.

Eating **healthy fats** is like giving your body a high-five! These fats, found in yummy things like avocados, nuts, and olive oil, are superstars when it comes to keeping us feeling great. They're not just tasty but also help our hearts stay happy by lowering bad cholesterol and reducing the risk of heart problems. Plus, they're like brain food—they support our noggin's power, helping us stay sharp and focused. Oh, and did I mention they're great for our skin and help us absorb important nutrients? So, next time you're reaching for a snack, go for those good fats—they'll keep you feeling awesome inside and out!

Most know that weight loss is 80% diet and 20% exercise. To get help with what to eat, this website is the best I've run into. Give it a try EatThis.com

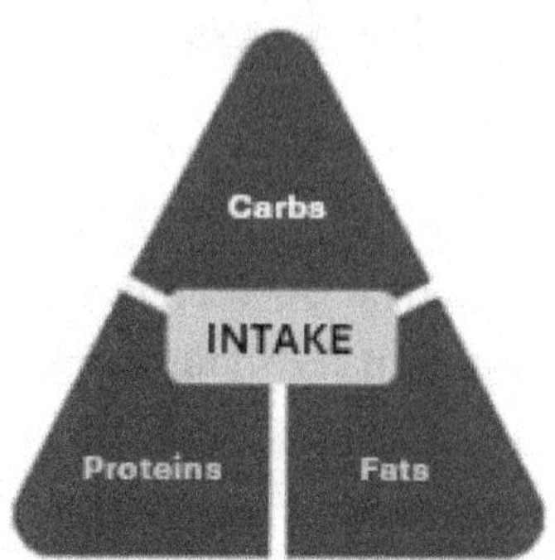
Carbs
INTAKE
Proteins
Fats

Carbs

Let's embark on a delicious journey through the world of carbs – because not all carbs are created equal! When it comes to fueling our bodies, it's essential to distinguish between the good carbs that keep us energized and satisfied and the not-so-good carbs that leave us feeling sluggish and hangry.

Good carbs – the unsung heroes of the food pyramid. These wholesome gems are packed with fiber, vitamins, and minerals, providing a slow and steady release of energy to keep us feeling full and satisfied. Think of whole grains like oats, quinoa, and brown rice, as well as fruits and veggies like apples, bananas, and leafy greens. These nutrient-dense delights are like the fuel that keeps our bodies humming along like a well-oiled machine, providing the energy we need to tackle whatever the day throws our way.

Bad carbs. These sneaky culprits might taste delicious, but they're like the villains of the food world, wreaking havoc on our waistlines and leaving us feeling sluggish and bloated. We're talking about refined carbs like white bread, sugary cereals, and processed snacks loaded with added sugars and empty calories. These tasty treats might provide a quick energy boost, but they're often followed by a crash that leaves us craving more – a vicious cycle that can sabotage our weight loss efforts and leave us feeling like we're stuck on a rollercoaster ride of highs and lows.

Last but certainly not least, let's chat about **the importance of balance.** While it's essential to limit our intake of bad carbs and opt for the good stuff whenever possible, it's also crucial not to demonize any particular food group. Carbs are an essential part of a healthy diet, providing the energy we need to fuel our workouts, support our brain function, and keep our bodies running smoothly.

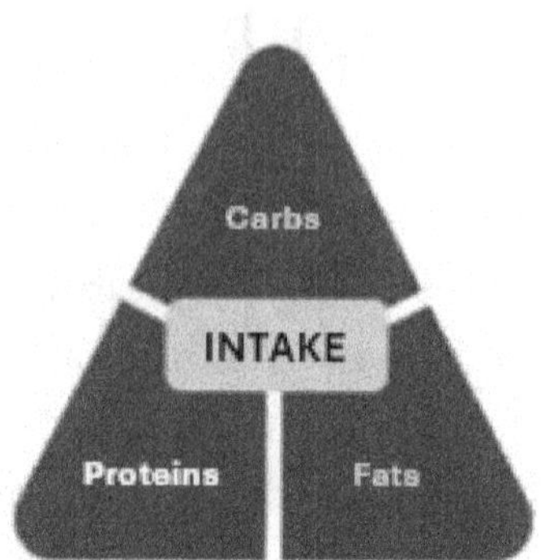
Carbs
INTAKE
Proteins
Fats

Proteins

Let's dig into the wonderful world of proteins – because not all proteins are created equal! Just like a superhero team, some proteins swoop in to save the day, while others might leave you feeling less than super. So, let's chat about the differences between good proteins that nourish your body and bad proteins that might not have your back.

Good proteins – the mighty defenders of your health and well-being. These powerhouse proteins are packed with essential amino acids, vitamins, and minerals, providing the building blocks your body needs to repair tissues, support muscle growth, and keep your immune system strong. Think of lean meats like chicken, turkey, and fish, as well as plant-based options like beans, lentils, and tofu. These nutrient-dense delights are like the loyal sidekicks that have your back, helping you feel satisfied and energized throughout the day.

Bad proteins. While they might taste delicious, these sneaky villains can wreak havoc on your health and sabotage your weight loss goals. We're talking about processed meats like bacon, sausage, and deli meats, as well as fried and breaded options that are loaded with unhealthy fats and excess calories. These tasty temptations might provide a quick burst of flavor, but they're often accompanied by a slew of negative side effects, including weight gain, inflammation, and an increased risk of chronic diseases like heart disease and diabetes.

The importance of balance. While it's essential to choose good proteins that nourish your body and support your health goals, it's also crucial not to demonize any particular food group. Protein is an essential part of a balanced diet, providing the energy and nutrients your body needs to thrive.

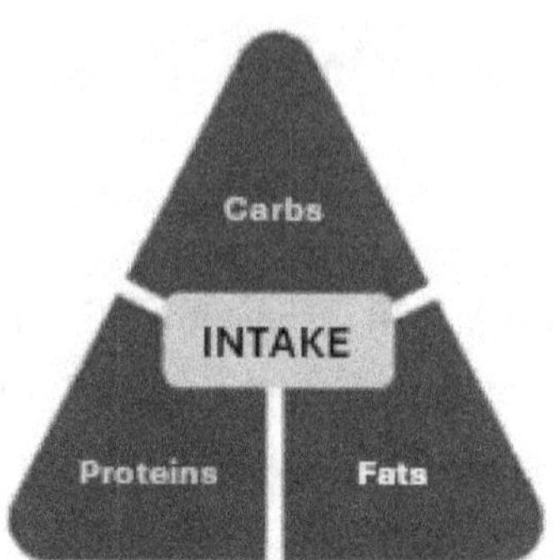

Carbs
INTAKE
Proteins
Fats

Fats

Let's dive into the flavorful world of fats – because not all fats are created equal! While some fats are like superheroes, swooping in to support our health and well-being, others might be more like sneaky villains, wreaking havoc on our waistlines and heart health. So, let's chat about the differences between healthy fats that nourish your body and unhealthy fats that might not have your back.

Healthy fats – the unsung heroes of the culinary kingdom. These mighty fats are like the golden ticket to better health, providing a host of benefits for your body and mind. Think of avocados, nuts, seeds, and fatty fish like salmon and trout – these delicious delights are packed with omega-3 fatty acids, vitamins, and minerals that support heart health, brain function, and overall well-being. Plus, healthy fats help keep you feeling full and satisfied, making them a key player in any balanced diet.

Unhealthy fats. These sneaky culprits might taste delicious, but they're like the villains of the food world, lurking in processed and fried foods and ready to wreak havoc on your health. We're talking about trans fats and saturated fats, which can raise your LDL cholesterol levels and increase your risk of heart disease and stroke. From greasy fast food to packaged snacks and baked goods, these unhealthy fats can be found lurking in all sorts of tasty treats – but don't let their tempting flavors fool you. When it comes to your health, it's best to enjoy these indulgences in moderation.

Now **the importance of balance**. While it's essential to limit your intake of unhealthy fats and opt for the good stuff whenever possible, it's also crucial not to fear fats altogether. Fat is an essential nutrient that plays a vital role in hormone production, nutrient absorption, and energy storage, so it's important to include a variety of healthy fats in your diet.

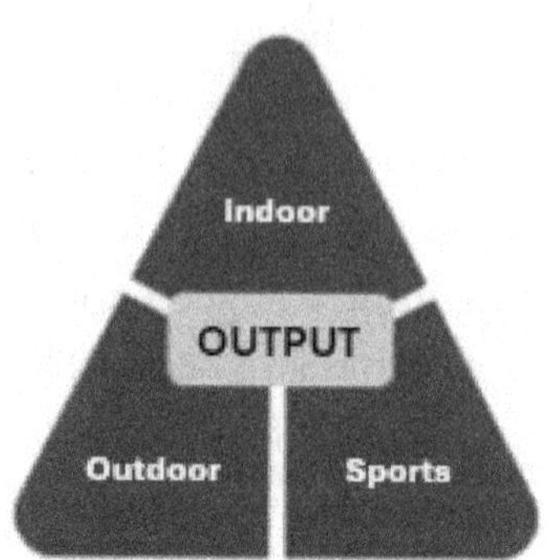
Indoor
OUTPUT
Outdoor
Sports

OUTPUT

Let's lace up our sneakers and hit the pavement because cardio workouts are like the secret sauce for maintaining a healthy weight! Whether you're dancing to your favorite tunes, hitting the trails for a jog, or pedaling away on a stationary bike, cardio exercises get your heart pumping and your sweat glands working overtime.

Cardio workouts **torch those calories** like nobody's business. When you're huffing and puffing through a heart-pounding session of cardio, your body becomes a calorie-burning machine, torching those pesky pounds and helping you maintain a healthy weight. Plus, cardio exercises elevate your heart rate and rev up your metabolism, helping you burn calories long after your workout is over. So, if you're looking to shed some extra pounds and keep them off for good, cardio workouts are your new best friend.

Next up, let's chat about the **heart-healthy benefits** of cardio exercises. Your ticker is like the engine that keeps your body running smoothly, and cardio workouts are like a tune-up for your heart. When you engage in regular cardio exercise, you strengthen your heart muscle, improve circulation, and lower your risk of heart disease and stroke. Plus, cardio workouts help regulate blood pressure, cholesterol levels, and blood sugar, keeping your heart in tip-top shape and your risk of chronic disease at bay.

Finally, let's talk about the **mood-boosting benefits** of cardio workouts. Ever heard of the "runner's high"? It's not just a myth – it's science! When you engage in cardio exercise, your brain releases feel-good chemicals like endorphins and serotonin, leaving you feeling happier, more relaxed, and less stressed. Plus, cardio workouts help improve sleep quality, boost energy levels, and enhance cognitive function, keeping your mind sharp and your spirits high. So, whether you're chasing that runner's high or dancing away your worries, cardio workouts are the key to maintaining a healthy weight and a happy heart.

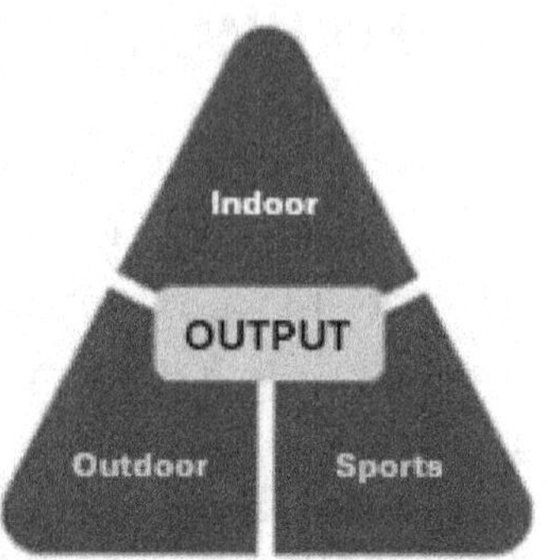
Indoor
OUTPUT
Outdoor
Sports

Indoor

Get ready to break a sweat without even stepping foot outside! Here's a list of indoor cardio exercises that'll have you feeling the burn and loving every minute of it:

- **Jumping Jacks:** Start with a classic! Jumping jacks are a fantastic full-body workout that gets your heart pumping and your muscles engaged. Plus, they're super fun to do, making them the perfect warm-up exercise.
- **High Knees:** Get those knees up! This high-energy exercise is like running in place, but with an added twist – lifting your knees as high as you can with each step. It's a great way to improve your cardiovascular fitness and build strength in your legs.
- **Burpees:** Love 'em or hate 'em, burpees are one of the most effective full-body exercises out there. Start in a standing position, then squat down, kick your legs back into a plank position, do a push-up, jump your feet back to your hands, and explode into a jump. It's like a mini workout all on its own!
- **Jump Rope:** Who says jump ropes are just for kids? Grab a rope and get jumping! It's a fantastic cardio workout that also helps improve coordination and agility. Plus, you can do it just about anywhere – no fancy equipment required!
- **Dancing:** Crank up your favorite tunes and let loose on the dance floor – or, you know, your living room. Dancing is not only a blast, but it's also a fantastic cardio workout that gets your heart rate up and your body moving in all the right ways.
- **Stair Climbing:** If you have stairs at home, put them to good use! Climbing stairs is a killer cardio workout that targets your legs, glutes, and core. You can mix things up by doing single steps, double steps, or even hopping up and down for an added

challenge.

- **Shadow Boxing:** Channel your inner Rocky and throw some punches! Shadow boxing is a fantastic way to get your heart rate up while also improving your coordination and strength. Plus, it's a great stress reliever – just imagine you're punching away all your worries!

So, whether you're looking to shake up your workout routine or just burn off some extra energy on a rainy day, these indoor cardio exercises are sure to do the trick. Get ready to sweat, smile, and feel fantastic!

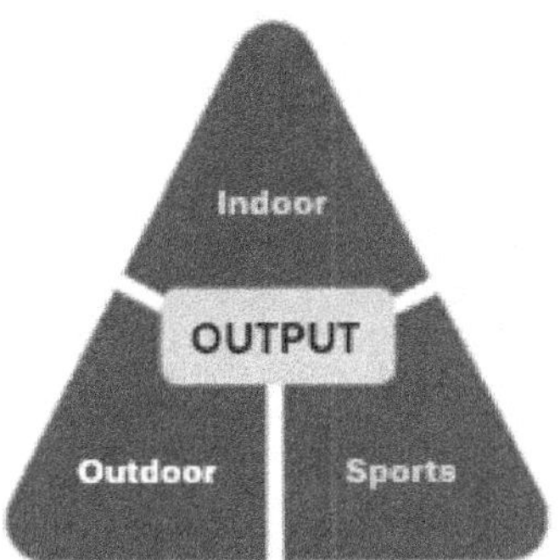

Indoor
OUTPUT
Outdoor
Sports

Outdoor

It's time to take your workout outdoors and enjoy some fresh air while breaking a sweat. Here's a list of fun and effective outdoor cardio exercises to help you maintain a healthy weight and have a blast while doing it:

- **Running or Jogging:** Lace up those sneakers and hit the pavement! Whether you prefer a leisurely jog around the neighborhood or a heart-pumping sprint through the park, running is a fantastic way to burn calories, boost your mood, and improve your cardiovascular fitness.
- **Cycling:** Dust off your bike and hit the trails for a scenic ride in the great outdoors. Cycling is not only a fantastic cardio workout that targets your legs and glutes, but it's also a low-impact exercise that's easy on the joints. Plus, you get to enjoy the beauty of nature as you pedal along.
- **Hiking:** Explore the great outdoors and get your heart rate up with a hike through the wilderness. Whether you're trekking through rugged terrain or meandering along a scenic trail, hiking is a fantastic way to burn calories, build strength, and connect with nature.
- **Swimming:** Dive into your nearest pool, lake, or ocean and enjoy a refreshing swim in the great outdoors. Swimming is a low-impact, full-body workout that's gentle on the joints and great for cardiovascular health. Plus, it's a fantastic way to cool off on a hot summer day!
- **Jump Rope:** Take your jump rope outside and skip your way to a healthier you! Jumping rope is a fantastic cardio workout that improves coordination, agility, and cardiovascular fitness. Plus, it's a fun and inexpensive way to get your heart pumping.
- **Rowing:** If you're near a body of water, why not try your hand

at rowing? Whether you're in a kayak, canoe, or rowboat, rowing is a fantastic full-body workout that targets your arms, back, and core while providing an excellent cardiovascular workout.

- **Outdoor Circuit Training:** Set up a circuit of outdoor exercises in your backyard or local park and get ready for a full-body workout. Include exercises like jumping jacks, squats, lunges, push-ups, and burpees, and alternate between each exercise for a high-intensity cardio workout that will leave you feeling energized and accomplished.

So, whether you prefer the open road, the tranquil waters, or the rugged trails, there's an outdoor cardio exercise for everyone. Get outside, soak up some sunshine, and enjoy the many benefits of exercising in the great outdoors!

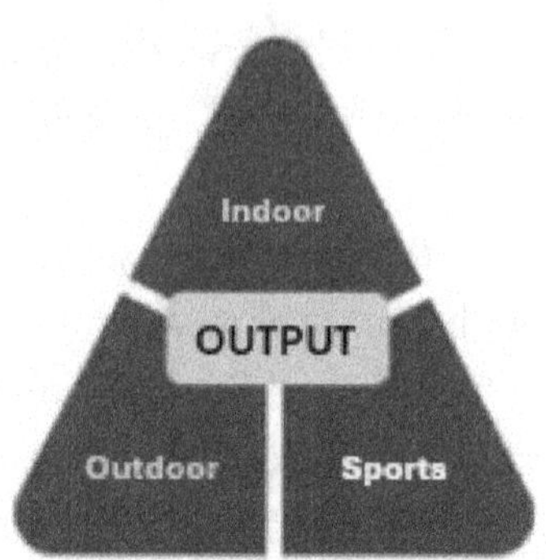
Indoor
OUTPUT
Outdoor
Sports

Sports

Here are some sport activities that'll keep your heart pumping and your muscles engaged:

- **Soccer:** Kick it up a notch with a game of soccer! Whether you're dribbling down the field, passing to teammates, or sprinting towards the goal, soccer is a fantastic cardio workout that improves agility, endurance, and cardiovascular fitness.
- **Basketball:** Shoot some hoops and break a sweat with a game of basketball. With its fast-paced nature and constant movement up and down the court, basketball is a fantastic cardio workout that also improves coordination, agility, and strength.
- **Tennis:** Grab your racket and hit the courts for a game of tennis. Whether you're serving up aces, rallying with your opponent, or sprinting to chase down a ball, tennis is a fantastic cardio workout that also improves agility, balance, and hand-eye coordination.
- **Volleyball:** Bump, set, and spike your way to a healthier you with a game of volleyball. Whether you're serving up serves, diving for digs, or spiking the ball over the net, volleyball is a fantastic cardio workout that also improves strength, flexibility, and teamwork.
- **Rugby:** Get ready to tackle and scrum your way to victory with a game of rugby. With its intense physicality and non-stop action, rugby is a fantastic cardio workout that also improves strength, endurance, and mental toughness.
- **Hockey:** Lace up your skates and hit the ice for a game of hockey. Whether you're skating up and down the rink, passing to teammates, or taking shots on goal, hockey is a fantastic cardio workout that also improves balance, coordination, and

agility.

- **Ultimate Frisbee:** Grab a Frisbee and hit the field for a game of ultimate Frisbee. With its fast-paced gameplay and constant movement, ultimate Frisbee is a fantastic cardio workout that also improves agility, speed, and teamwork.

So, whether you prefer kicking, dribbling, serving, spiking, tackling, skating, or throwing, there's a sport out there that'll keep your heart pumping and your muscles engaged. Get out there, have fun, and reap the many cardio benefits of playing sports!

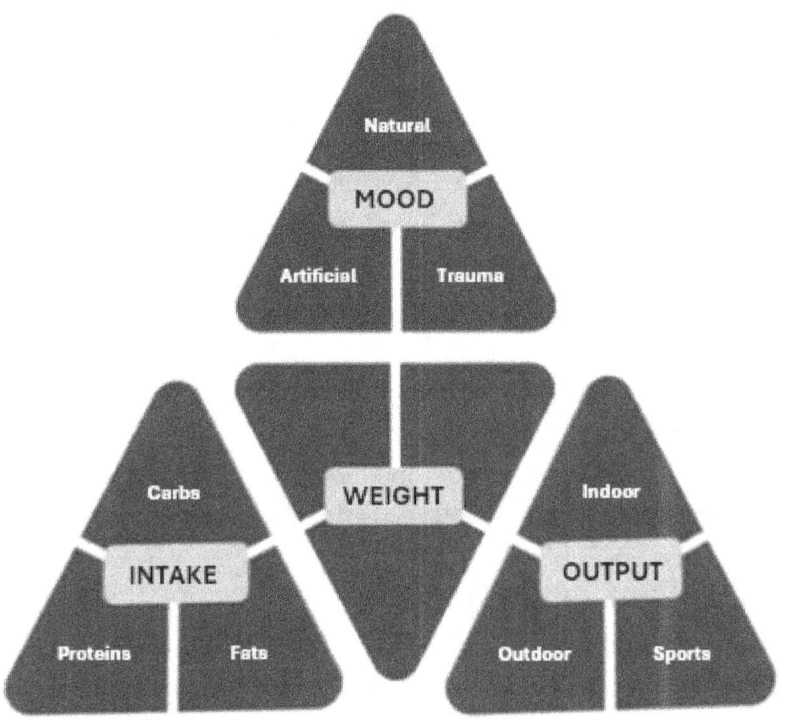
Natural
MOOD
Artificial
Trauma
Carbs
WEIGHT
Indoor
INTAKE
OUTPUT
Proteins
Fats
Outdoor
Sports

SUMMARY

Let's take a stroll down the path of healthy living and explore the differences between an active lifestyle and a sedentary lifestyle. Picture this: one is like a bustling city street filled with energy and movement, while the other is more like a cozy couch nestled in front of the TV. Let's break it down!

First up, we have **the active lifestyle** – the vibrant, bustling hub of physical activity and energy. When you lead an active lifestyle, you're like a dynamo, constantly on the move and making the most of every moment. Whether you're hitting the gym, going for a run, or taking a brisk walk around the neighborhood, physical activity is woven into the fabric of your daily routine. Not only does this keep your body strong and healthy, but it also boosts your mood, improves your sleep, and enhances your overall quality of life.

On the flip side, we have **the sedentary lifestyle** – the cozy, comfortable haven of relaxation and rest. When you lead a sedentary lifestyle, you're like a sloth, spending the majority of your time sitting or lying down with minimal physical activity. Whether you're binge-watching your favorite TV show, scrolling through social media, or lounging on the couch for hours on end, your body isn't getting the movement it needs to thrive. Not only can this lead to weight gain and poor physical health, but it can also increase your risk of chronic diseases like heart disease, diabetes, and even certain types of cancer.

But fear not, my friend, because **it's never too late to make a change!** By incorporating more physical activity into your daily routine – whether it's taking the stairs instead of the elevator, going for a walk during your lunch break, or trying out a new exercise class – you can reap the many benefits of an active lifestyle and say goodbye to the sedentary slump. So, lace up those sneakers, get moving, and embrace the wonderful world of health and vitality that awaits!

Invitation

Let's slow things down and savor the journey towards better health and fitness. Taking things slow with exercise isn't just a wise choice – it's like laying a sturdy foundation for a skyscraper. By starting at a comfortable pace and gradually building up your strength and endurance, you set yourself up for long-term success and **avoid the risk of burnout or injury.**

First and foremost, **taking things slow with exercise** allows your body to adjust and adapt to new movements and routines. Just like a delicate flower unfurling its petals, your muscles, joints, and cardiovascular system need time to acclimate to the demands of physical activity. By starting with gentle exercises and gradually increasing the intensity and duration over time, you give your body the opportunity to build strength, improve flexibility, and enhance endurance without overwhelming it.

Next, let's talk about **the mental aspect of taking things slow with exercise**. In a world that often glorifies extreme workouts and rapid transformations, it's easy to feel pressured to push yourself beyond your limits. But here's the thing – exercise should be enjoyable, not exhausting. By taking things slow and listening to your body's cues, you can cultivate a positive relationship with exercise and foster a sense of empowerment and self-confidence. Plus, by setting realistic goals and celebrating your progress along the way, you'll stay motivated and inspired to keep going.

Last but certainly not least, let's chat about the importance of **sustainability**. Rome wasn't built in a day, and neither is a healthy lifestyle. By taking things slow with exercise, you create habits that are sustainable for the long haul. Instead of burning out after a few weeks of intense workouts, you'll find yourself settling into a rhythm that feels comfortable and enjoyable. Plus, by gradually increasing the intensity and variety of your workouts over time, you'll continue to challenge yourself and experience new levels of strength, stamina, and vitality. So, whether you're taking your first steps on the path to fitness or embarking on a new exercise routine, remember to take it slow, savor the journey, and celebrate every small victory along the way. Your body and mind will thank you for it!

When you're with someone who is sharing their struggles with you...just smile at him/her and give them one of these. He/she will ask "What is that?" Then simply reply "Life Works in Threes."

Other titles coming out:

- Life Struggles?
- Abundance Struggles?
- Parenting Struggles?
- Romance Struggles?
- Purpose Struggles?
- Happiness Struggles?
- Sales Struggles?
- Speaker Struggles?
- Time Struggles?
- Network Struggles?
- Marriage Struggles?
- Divorce Struggles?
- Money Struggles?
- Career Struggles?
- Dating Struggles?
- Caretaker Struggles?
- Forgiveness Struggles?
- Grieving Struggles?
- Success Struggles?
- Golf Struggles?
- Workplace Struggles?
- Stress Struggles?
- Shame/Guilt Struggles?
- Addiction Struggles?

Quotes about Weight

"Take care of your body. It's the only place you have to live." - Jim Rohn

"It's not what you're eating. It's what's eating you." - Janet Greeson

"The groundwork of all happiness is health." - Leigh Hunt

"Weight loss is not a physical challenge, it's a mental one." - Unknown

"You are what you eat." - Many people say this

Remember,

When you get right down to it,

Life is about making choices.

Every day, all day long, that's what we do.

- *We chose to get out of bed or not.*
- *We chose to clean up or not.*
- *We chose what to eat all day.*
- *We chose to exercise or not.*
- *We chose to go to work or not.*
- *We chose to do a good job or not.*
- *We chose to come home or not.*
- *We chose to watch TV or do something constructive.*
- *We chose to bed at a decent hour or not.*

And the next day...we start all over again.

What is the meaning of this? Get good at choosing.

Before you can get good at choosing though...you need to understand how life works in threes.

When someone is struggling with a particular area or two, chances are they are "out of balance" with how life works. How does life work? Life works in threes.

If you're interested in personal topics like life, health, money or business topics like sales, time management and public speaking...TRYUNE WORKS! can shed some light on creating success in those areas.

The definition of TRIUNE is a group of three things; united. Being three in one, such as - humans are *mental, physical* and *spiritual beings.* The word TRYUNE is a play of the word TRIUNE, encouraging all to try this concept and help eliminate struggling unnecessarily.

LifeWorksInThrees.com

www.ingramcontent.com/pod-product-compliance
Lightning Source LLC
Chambersburg PA
CBHW070316160726
47999CB00003B/1043